Reflections of Light

Poetic Companions for the Journey with God

Cindy Luukkonen

Dear Jesus,

I want You to know how Your words, the very words in this book, have impacted me:
Your Words are precious gifts that come at just the right time.
Your Words give me hope in the darkest moments.
Your Words draw me deeper into that place of seeing You at work in my life
*   — even in the dark and seemingly unknown places.*
Your Words give purpose and meaning to my life.
Your Words help me to stand and find my sure and steady foundation found only in You.
Your Words encourage me to press on and press in to the deepest place of knowing You
*   and Your great and awesome love for me.*
Your Words bring me to that unshakeable place that is near and dear to Your heart
*   — that place where I am rooted and grounded in You.*
Your Words are able to satisfy even the deepest longings of my heart.
Your Words bring healing and light.
Your Words are worship to my soul.
May Your Words, living in me, touch others even as Your Words have touched and changed my life.
Dearest Jesus — You are truly my hope and my delight.
Precious Jesus — my Savior and Friend.

CONTENTS

MORNING — NEW BEGINNINGS

Psalm 143:8 NIV
Let the morning bring me word of Your unfailing love,
for I have put my trust in You.

Awake Now, My Spirit

Awake now, my spirit, come and arise.
Connect with my God; He has a surprise.
He's waiting and ready to speak to my heart.
Be open to Him; let Him trigger a spark.

Fill up in His presence 'til I overflow —
A fountain of water will spring up, *I know*.
Oh, what a joy to be near to my Lord.
Arise, O my spirit, come now, be restored.

Awake now, my spirit; come and arise.
Connect to my brother and sister through eyes.
Through your eyes I see some reflections of me.
Connected together, awakened and free.

Connect to my past to learn from my ways;
The road I have followed gives wisdom today.
Let me go forth, trusting in You to lead.
Your will be done; each step, I proceed.

Awake now, my spirit, come and arise.
Connect with my Self — be honest and wise.
Conviction will come; let it stop me from sin,
Before I jump in and let it begin.

Speak to the child in me: what do I need?
Fill up in that place, so that I can be freed.
What's at the heart of it? What can it be?
Show me what's covered up inside of me.

O Spirit, arise in my slumbering soul.
Quicken my spirit; come make me whole.
Connect me to God, to others as well;
In You I find life, and in You I dwell.

Sunrise

A new day's begun
With rising the sun.

The God of creation
Is in this location —

From here I can see
His smile upon me.

Glowing with splendor,
Gracefully tender —

Creating such brilliance,
Shows up as resilience.

This sight of His glory
He's launching His story.

Beginning today —
His magnificent way!

New Day

Awake, oh sleeper, rise from your slumber.
Awaken your heart; it's time to uncover.
The promise of God, it's yours for the taking.
Let it come in, as daylight is breaking.

Fill up with the truth, then let it define —
Each word upon word; and line upon line.
Whose you are — let it into your being,
His Word, His promise, and all He is seeing.

Reach out and go forth, for it is a new day.
Follow and run with Him all of the way,
Aware what He's doing and all He's about,
For surely, you'll see Him there on your route,
    Then lift up your voice — rejoice with a shout!

The Way to God

How do I find more time in my day —
To live and to move and just to obey?
Devoted to you, this is the way:
Simply begin — take time now to pray.

How do I know just where You are now?
Show me the way and what You're about.
Here in this place, I need to know how —
To hear Your voice and follow Your route.

How do I listen and quiet my soul?
Then let You come in and give You control,
Surrendering all, that is my goal —
To glorify You, Your name to extol!

Silence

I come to the silence — to listen and hear,
To lean on the One who makes all things clear.
The silence — it opens, unclouds my ear,
When I come to the One, most treasured and dear.

In silence, He speaks to my heart today —
Words that I hear now show me the way
To live in this moment and not far away.
His words come softly; there is no delay.

This word is for me and maybe for you;
For deep in my heart, I know it is true.
It's just what I need to know and pursue.
In silence, it comes and clears up my view.

The light burns away all that's unknown;
It clears away all to see what is shown.
In silence, the moving of God can be known —
When I wait in His presence with Him all alone.

Wind of the Spirit

Wind of the Spirit —
Blow upon me.
Up to the heights
Where I can move free.

There on the heights,
Your beauty I see.
All of Your glory
As far as the sea.

Moved by the Spirit
Living in me;
Your way is clear.
Wouldn't you agree?

Wind of the Spirit —
Move within me.
Take me to heights
Where I am near Thee.

Alignment

Come, Holy Spirit, help me align
All that's within me by Your design.
Clear out the things I need to refine
So I can live with Your ways in mine.

    I speak to my spirit: come into a line
    Under the Holy One — that's the design.
    Follow Him quickly, then let Him define
    All I can be, what He would assign.

    I speak to my soul: follow behind.
    Let Spirit lead — heart, will, and mind.
    Follow the way; in surrender, you find
    The way for my soul to not be confined.

    I speak to my body: you cannot define
    Nor can you lead, for that's not divine.
    Give up your ways, then let's redefine.
    Stay in this order; don't cross the line.

From here I go forth, always in line.
Ready to live in God's great design.
Here in a place, where I know I will shine —
That place in the Spirit; it truly is mine!

Prayer

It all begins where
I'm seated with Christ.
Near to His throne
With Him on the heights.

Here in His presence
He's with me today.
His power and glory
Moves mountains away.

The armor, it keeps
All things in their place.
Authority wins —
It opens the gates.

The weapons we use
The world has not known.
Divine power moves;
His glory is shown.

So here's where I stand —
With power in Christ
To shift atmospheres,
To make all things right.

No challenge is there
That He cannot change.
All things possible,
By His great exchange.

The power of prayer
From heaven above
Brings heaven to earth —
His infinite love!

Thankfulness

Today, I am thankful for all that You give,
Thankful to You that in this time I live.

To live in *today* is to live in Your way —
Surrounded by goodness, Your love on display.

Thankfulness keeps my heart full of joy,
For this I give thanks that I can employ.

When all that I see is worthy of praise,
Then I am thankful for all of my days.

God has been faithful, so loving and kind;
Today, I am thankful in Him I can find:

A way to let thankfulness be in the start,
Each day to let thankfulness rule in my heart.

Formation

Each day I come to the Word to pray,
Hoping to grow in some small way.
Changed by the truth — let it stay,
So I can be more like Him each day.

Let Christ be formed in me today —
Living by truth, not wanting to sway.
Molded I am as the potter's clay;
Wholly transformed — without delay.
Formation happens when I obey.

Quiet

Quiet is peaceful; Quiet is rest.
It is in Quiet
    I hear God the best.

Quiet is leaning; Quiet is here.
It is in Quiet
    I open my ear.

Quiet is listening; Quiet is true.
It is in Quiet
    I hear what to do.

Quiet is seeing; Quiet is made.
It is in Quiet
    I am not afraid.

Quiet is speaking; Quiet is clear.
It is in Quiet
    I see God appear.

Quiet is silence; Quiet is still.
It is in Quiet
    I discover God's will.

Quiet is peaceful; Quiet is rest.
It is in Quiet
    I hear God the best.

In the Silence

In the silence,
He is far yet near.
I wait.
I listen.
Your word I hear.

The weight of Your presence.
I feel.
I see.
Such glorious beauty,
Wrapped all around me.

A blanket of love,
Here in this place.
I listen.
I wait.
You open the gate.

Rest

Rest is His love;
Come and abide.
Sit at His feet;
Gaze in His eyes.

Rest is a place
Where strivings must cease.
Come and enjoy
His perfect peace.

Rest is a time
When all is done.
Work is completed;
The race has been won.

Rest is my peace
Where fullness abounds.
Here in His presence —
In rest, I am found.

Moment in Time

Capture this moment
Before it's too late.
Slow down; don't hurry!
Just sit here and wait.

Be still and listen;
Time will not delay.
Don't miss this moment
To live in today.

Your gift is your time —
Cherish its display!

Waiting

Wait in the quiet and then I will hear —
The calling of God to come ever near.
Deep in my soul, find what wrestles within.
Hidden inside; it's time to begin.

Waiting is active, no time to be still;
Working things out, letting go of my will.
All things that trouble my weary heart,
Let them all go; get ready to start.

Waiting is bringing contentment to me,
So I can live in myself and just be
I am now certain this one thing I know:
Waiting is good, for it helps me to grow.

When waiting has finished its work within me,
Then I will live, and then I'll be free.
To be in this place where I'm satisfied,
Near to my God where I'm fully alive!

MIDDAY — WALKING IN THE LIGHT

1 John 1:7 ESV
If we walk in the light, as He is in the light, we have fellowship with one another,
and the blood of Jesus His Son cleanses us from all sin.

Pilgrims

We are pilgrims on a journey.
Walk with me; I am going there, too.
Far ahead, our destination —
Ancient steps lead us to You.

Each day brings us so much closer
To the place where we have sight.
Over hills and through the valleys,
We go forward in Your light.

The journey's long and sometimes weary,
Yet You come each day anew.
Give us strength to go the distance —
Onward, upward, nearer You.

Journey to New

Questions unanswered,
All the unknowns —
What is the future
That I will be shown?

On this journey,
I follow Your lead —
Begin to slow down,
Let go of my speed.

I'm here to listen,
To walk by Your side.
I'm changing my pace;
It helps me abide.

How will this happen?
And when will I know
All that You've done —
Will it even show?

How will this change me —
To walk here with You?
To go on this journey?
To see a new view?

This is for certain—
I will be made new!

Pilgrimage

What from my past do I leave behind
To lighten my load? Now I must decide.
The journey is long, so I must prepare
By counting the steps that lead to somewhere.

What will I take for the journey each day,
To carry along, to use on my way?
What will appear on this journey for me —
A new way to live? A new way to be?

From steps others walked, I follow their lead.
Receiving from them what they have decreed.
Where will this journey of my life now go?
All that is certain, Your way I must know.
    This pilgrim's journey — formed long, long ago.

Rhythms

Inspired by walking a pilgrimage in Scotland

Rhythms of walking here in this place;
Creating rhythms opens the space.
Letting God in to then see His face.
Rhythms of mercy, rhythms of grace.

Rhythms of hearts beating as one,
Listen for rhythms that have begun.
Follow their lead, then let them run
Until they're complete and your work is done.

Rhythms of silence waiting to hear.
What is the rhythm that shall appear?
Listen so closely until it is clear.
His words will come softly into your ear.

Rhythms of voices here can be found
Connecting our hearts; you hear the sound.
Grace upon grace, His mercies abound.
Walking together, firmly on the ground.

New rhythms created, inside and out.
A pilgrim's journey is what it's about.
So from this place, without any doubt,
I go with God, for He has a new route.

Run With Me

Freely I've called you, freely to run;
Open before me the time has begun —
To run with the Spirit to heights unknown;
Follow the pathway you have been shown.

No assist needed to stay the course;
All you've been given, you know the source.
Keep in your lane, and do not fear.
You know the way; it's straight and it's clear.

Run, quickly, run! In the fast lane, we go;
Pass all that's hidden and all that goes slow.
Keep moving forward, unhindered by all;
Run with Me quickly — there's no time to stall.

Places to go in the Spirit with Me;
It's so exciting to run and be free.
Come now with Me; this time is for you
To go to the place with a beautiful view
Where we can meet here — just Me and you.

Hebrews 12:1-2 ESV
Therefore, since we are surrounded by so great a cloud of witnesses, let us also lay aside every weight and sin which clings so closely, and let us run with endurance the race that is set before us, looking to Jesus, the founder and perfecter of our faith, who for the joy that was set before Him endured the cross, despising the shame, and is seated at the right hand of the throne of God.

Promised Land

He parted the waters
For me to walk through.
The dry land appeared —
A pathway made new.

I see in this land
His promise to me;
He's opened a way —
A new life to be.

This land, it is flowing;
His goodness abounds.
This place in the Spirit
Where life will be found.

So here I now stand,
About to go in —
To cross to the side
Where I've never been.

I'm here, and I'm ready.
My response — let's begin!

Crossings

Written during a pilgrimage in Scotland to Holy Island

Crossing the pathways intersecting time,
The ancient paths I'm here to find.
The way to walk as others have gone,
To learn from their journey that moves me on.

Crossing through gates, then closing the door
To all that is past; I'll look back no more.
Forward and onward, through valleys and hills,
To be near to His heart, to be closer still.

Crossing the bridges, swaying in the wind —
Beyond solid ground, a new place begins.
Feeling unsafe — where will this lead?
Yet trusting Him always; He knows what I need.

Crossing through grasses, pathways are hidden;
Keep moving forward, completing the mission.
Crossing through fields of ripening grain,
Planted as seeds with so much to gain.

Crossing the rivers, even small streams —
Each one is leading to dreams I have dreamed:
Of all He has for me and all I will be.
When my life is finished, I'll fully be me.

Crossing the heights, such steep steps to climb.
Tired and weary — will I make it in time?
No need to worry; He's leading me on.
Closer to Him, that's where I belong.

Crossing the tracks to the other side,
But first, I must ask when the timing is right.
Inviting me in, He's there at the gate,
Open before me — there's no need to wait.

One final crossing for me to now bear;
This one will lead to His promises there.
The crossing's before me, without delay,
I'm here; I'm ready! Today is the day!

Where will this lead me at this very time?
Through so many crossings; they're waiting in line.
Each one has beauty, and each one I'm shown
The way to beyond and how I have grown.

Each cross is a place to let go of old me
And die to the ways that I used to be.
This is my prayer, my very plea:
To find in the end, a new way to just be.

Prepare to Run

How far is Your reach,
O God of the seas?
Your hand is not short
To do as You please.

Submitted to You,
I follow Your lead.
You open the way
For plans to succeed.

Stretch me, O God,
Beyond what I see,
Out into the dark;
What's open for me?

Lengthen my cords,
Then strengthen my stakes.
New things You're preparing;
It is no mistake.

Expanding is coming;
You're making a way.
Foundations are laid
Of ways that must stay.

Be ready and waiting;
The time will be shown.
From here to go forth,
Fully into unknown.

Prepare and be ready;
Swiftly, it will come.
When all is in place,
Together we run!

Times

Times and seasons, they come and they go.
What is my time in the Spirit to know?
Walking beside You keeps me in line,
All just to know Your heart at this time.

A time to plant and a time to reap,
A time to gather and then to keep,
A time to mourn and a time to weep,
Then time for joy, found out in the deep.

A time to love in all its embrace,
A time for God to fill up my space,
A time to know and seek God's face,
Then time to run with Him in this race.

A time to hold and a time to let go,
A time to speak and a time to be known,
A time for peace where His love is shown;
Now is the time, for I'm not alone.

Restart

Open my ears to hear what You're saying,
So I can be led in this prayer I am praying:
Dear God, l draw near;
Your voice I must hear
To silence the fear
That shakes me apart
From deep in my heart —
I need a restart.

Open my eyes to see all Your beauty.
Around me and in me, You come to pursue me.
Dear God, show to me
Just what Your eyes see
Of all that can be.
To see what's apart
That changes my heart —
I need a restart.

Open my heart to feel what You're feeling;
Compassion and love are always appealing.
Dear God, make a way,
What I need each day —
A love to convey
That sets me apart.
Your love in my heart
Brings me a restart.

Communion

On the night of betrayal, He showed me His love
In breaking the bread sent from heaven above.
The cup of His blood, He poured out for me.
All this so that I am eternally free.

Eat of His body, broken for me,
Suffered and pierced on an old rugged tree.
The truth that I hear is that I'm now complete —
Sin, sickness, and death, you are obsolete.

Drink of His blood poured out for me,
The blood of His life, now living and free.
This great exchange — His life for mine,
How can it be? What a grand design!

Do this, *remember*, and keep in your heart,
Especially when you need a restart.
Let it come in with strength from above.
Taste of His goodness; it's what He's made of.
This is His gift to you — wrapped in His love.

Matthew 26:26-29 ESV
Now as they were eating, Jesus took bread, and after blessing it broke it and gave it to the disciples, and said, "Take, eat; this is my body." And He took a cup, and when He had given thanks He gave it to them, saying, "Drink of it, all of you, for this is my blood of the covenant, which is poured out for many for the forgiveness of sins. I tell you I will not drink again of this fruit of the vine until that day when I drink it new with you in my Father's kingdom."

Changed by His Love

Open my heart; let His light come in.
Open it wide; reveal what is sin.
See every corner hidden from sight;
Bring it out fully into the light.

Clean up the mess that's buried within,
So I can be free to let life begin.
What's in my heart that needs Your touch?
I need to know — You love me so much.

Line upon line, let Your truth be known;
For me to hear clearly — Your way to be shown.
All You have for me; let it now be.
Today I go forth in fullness — free.

Truth is the One who lives by my side;
With You, I now live and always abide.
Where will this lead? In You, I will know;
Your love will be with me wherever I go.

Oh, what a joy to be changed by Your love —
Forgiven and free to live from above.
Your nearness to me is all I desire;
Lord, take me with You, higher and higher.

All praise to my God, whose blessings I know.
You've brought me so far for You love me so.
What more do You have? It's You I pursue.
With passion I seek to live life anew.
Oh Jesus, my Jesus, I'm grateful to You!

Be Childlike, Carefree

Today, I am calling
For you to be
Full of joy,
Childlike, carefree!

Run with Me,
Then you'll be blessed;
Now is the time,
The season of rest.

Lift off the burdens;
Hand them to Me.
No need to carry;
Be Childlike, carefree!

Seize the moment;
Enjoy the day.
Live in My presence.
Follow My way.

Here in this moment,
I draw you near —
To see, to feel;
There's no need to fear.

Come to this place,
Near to My heart.
I am with you;
We're never apart.

Greater am I
Than all in the world.
Find peace; find joy
With heart unfurled.

This is My gift,
Today receive Me;
Be filled with My life,
Childlike, Carefree!

Yours Alone

Jesus, take all of me near to Your heart;
That's where I dwell — no, never apart.

You are my life, my joy, and my prize;
Into Your presence, to look in Your eyes.

Fill up in me, 'til I overflow.
Let it spill out; to Jesus I go.

Power and glory, let it be known;
O Jesus, my Jesus, I am Yours alone.

One Thing

One thing I need,
This that I seek:
To quiet my heart,
With Jesus to speak.

For in the quiet,
Distractions let go.
This one thing is there —
His peace, I will know.

Out in the world,
It all comes apart.
His safety is found
Deep in my heart.

Many things calling,
But one thing is clear —
A longing to live
With One I hold dear.

Today I will choose
To let it all go.
To focus on One.
This one thing I know.

Psalm 27:4 NIV
One thing I ask from the Lord, this only do I seek: that I may dwell in the house of the Lord all the days of my life, to gaze on the beauty of the Lord and to seek Him in his temple.

Draw Near to Me

Draw near to Me,
For I've opened the veil,
A place that's been hidden —
Come near and dwell.

Doors with their locks
Are now open inside;
This place near Me —
Come and abide.

A place near My heart
Is open for you.
I'm waiting right here;
Let Me show you what's true.

Come live in My truth
For all of your days.
There is a new way;
I am with you always.

My beautiful one,
You've captured My heart.
Our journey together
Has made a new start.
Now onward we go,
No, never apart.

Hebrews 10:19-22 TPT

And now we are brothers and sisters in God's family because of the blood of Jesus, and He welcomes us to come into the most holy sanctuary in the heavenly realm— boldly and without hesitation. For He has dedicated a new, life-giving way for us to approach God. For just as the veil was torn in two, Jesus' body was torn open to give us free and fresh access to Him! And since we now have a magnificent High Priest to welcome us into God's house, we come closer to God and approach Him with an open heart, fully convinced that nothing will keep us at a distance from Him. For our hearts have been sprinkled with blood to remove impurity, and we have been freed from an accusing conscience. Now we are clean, unstained, and presentable to God inside and out!

Thin Places

Thin places happen
When heaven draws near.
The veil is lifted;
His face appears.

Sweet words come softly,
His voice in my ear,
Whispering gently.
All things are made clear.

His presence — so sacred,
My heart knows He's near.
Divine and so holy —
His love is so dear.

Wordless Prayer

In quiet, I hear
You calling to me.
When deep calls to deep,
Your face I must see.

Rest here My child;
I'm here with you.
This is enough;
It's all you must do.

Your presence is sweet,
Refreshing delight.
Here in Your presence,
Your light becomes bright.

Longer and longing,
Your call is to come.
So now I must go,
Until I become.

Parable of the Sower

Scattered and sown — seeds fall to the ground.
Just where they land is where they are found.
Some on the hard and beaten-down path,
Snatched by the birds that come to attack.

Some fell on rocks where soil was thin —
No chance was there for growth to begin.
Scorched and withered without any root,
They died without life and bore no fruit.

Some fell among thorns that choked out life,
Stealing it all and producing such strife.
Yet some fell in soil and was nurtured with care —
Ready for seed; much fruit it will bear.

This is the soil that's tilled and prepared,
All by the Gardener — His love He has shared.
Listen to Him for He knows the way
To live in the garden, to bear fruit each day

Listen to hear, understand, and believe
All that is there for you to receive.
Tend to the garden within your own heart.
There in the soil the seed does its part:
Sprouting and growing, divine work of art.

The Garden Within

Take me back to the garden within,
Back to the place before there was sin.
Your cleansing blood says I am forgiven,
To walk with my God in the garden again.

Long time ago, before time began,
God made the world — a woman and man.
Perfect and holy, it was His plan.
Sin entered the garden, and so I was banned.

God made a way to redeem the lost,
Considered it all — even the cost.
A sacrifice made, once and for all,
Freely forgiven, this was His call.

The garden, it calls me: enter here.
His presence is sweet; I see it so clear.
Near to His heart this garden within,
His beauty restored — new life begins.

NIGHT — DARKNESS INTO LIGHT

Psalm 18:28 NIV
You, LORD, keep my lamp burning;
my God turns my darkness into light.

Winter Trees

Trees in the winter,
Exposed and laid bare;
Their shelter of leaves
Now scattered out there.

The trees that once were
So stately and strong
Appear to be dead.
Where do they belong?

Solitude calls me
From deep within —
Come here to this place
Of winter — come in.

Like barren, cold trees,
My heart comes to know
This place that is empty —
Where I can let go.

Worldly addictions
Once found in this place
No longer carry
Their need to embrace.

Here in the darkness
I'm learning to lean,
To rest in His silence
'Til His way is seen.

Like wintering trees
My life is forced down,
To go ever deeper —
Deep into the ground.

As roots go down deep,
To establish this place —
Where strength is now found
And weakness replaced.

For here in this place,
A new life is found —
To live and to move
From deep in the ground.

More settled and strong,
Resilient and free,
When winter's completed
Its work inside me.

For when spring abounds,
And surely it will,
Then here in this place,
A strong tree stands still.

Rooted and grounded,
Established in love,
Solid in virtues,
Hope springs from above.

Trees in the winter —
Laid bare and alone.
Something of beauty,
Comes from the unknown.

The Secret Place

In the darkness, the secret hides;
All alone, inside it resides.
Fear and shame keep all things in;
No one must see what's hidden within.

In that place, secluded alone,
Hidden away; it must not be known.
It's where I live and where I must go;
Just to feel safe — the safe place I know.

There in the darkness I can just be
Safe and secure, alone, just me.
No one to tell, so I hold it all in;
The secret is safe — safe within.

Coming from darkness into the light —
It's not so easy; I want to take flight.
But here I am; there must be a way.
Here at the start, I have something to say.

This secret place that's hidden inside —
Now I am ready, in You to confide.
Replace the darkness; let light come in.
God's healing touch; I feel it within.
The time is now ready, so let us begin.

Lament

Why am I so troubled inside?
Where I feel empty — I just want to hide.

Nothing seems right; no purpose is found.
Life is just living flat on the ground.

Sadness has come; it's stolen my heart.
Things have no meaning; I feel torn apart.

This I now know; for God is my hope.
He carries me up from this slippery slope.

Up to the place where life can be found.
Near to His heart; that place I'll abound.

Purpose and meaning one day will be clear;
When all is complete, by His side I am near.
     Where there will be no shedding of tears.

Burdens

Burdens I carry
Too heavy to bear,
Weighing me down
When climbing the stairs.

Slowly releasing,
I open my hands.
Burdens are lifted;
My grasp, it disbands.

His yoke is easy;
His burdens are light.
No need to worry;
I'm here in His sight.

Forward I travel
With lighter a load.
He took it away
To walk a new road.

No need to worry,
'Cause I'm in His care;
He carries it all —
My burdens to bear.

Rest here in this place;
It's all I can do,
When I rest in Him,
My load lightens, too.

The Wall

Here I am standing
In front of the wall.
How will I get through
When I am so small?

The wall is so high —
I know I can't climb
And to go under
Would take a long time.

Yet, my Father knows
Just what I should do.
He leads me forward;
He has a way through.

Each stone in the wall
Has something to tell,
For me to notice
Just what to dispel.

Some stones are my past
All covered with lies;
They hold me down
Beneath their disguise.

Some stones are anger,
Fear, shame, grief, and pain
If I let them go —
I have so much to gain.

For me at the wall,
My past is made peace.
All is forgiven;
I have been released.

For me at the wall,
I swallow my pride,
Learn to be humble
With God on my side.

For me at the wall,
Myself comes to die;
Now living for God,
Not centered on I.

For me at the wall,
I give up control,
Surrendering all
To live life as whole.

This time at the wall,
I start to know me
Without all the ways
That I used to be.

For when it is time
To go through the wall,
Then, I am ready
To answer the call.

God has been with me
He's my All-in-All!

Free and Clear

What does it take to get outside?
What's holding me back in this place I hide?
Broken and tattered and fallen apart.
Pieces are scattered; where do I start?

The wall seems so high; what will it take?
Remove all the stones; it's not a mistake.
Little holes in the wall provide just a peek
Into what is beyond and all that I seek.

Stones piled high, mortared with lies
That hold them together; it is no surprise.
Chipping away, piece by piece they fall;
One by one falling as down comes the wall.

Outside of the wall, the enemy waits.
He lurks and he barks; it's freedom he hates.
Yet You come beside me and lead me through,
You show me the door and just what to do.

I stand at this crossroads; what's next for me?
To get to the other side and be free.
It's here that I learn that I can command —
The power is there; just hold out my hand.

Freedom is there; I can see it in sight,
But first I must learn to wait for the light.
To go in too early would be such a fault;
I wait in Your presence for time to go out.

The waves of the Spirit are leading me on
Wherever You've called me, to go beyond,
Over my head where the Spirit now leads,
To places You've called — to scatter the seeds.

Then seeing beyond and all that is there,
I go forth from this place, completely aware
Of where I have been and where I am here —
To show others the way, to let walls disappear,
To live a new life — to be free and clear.

Road Construction

Around every corner
And down every turn,
There is construction
And something to learn.

Fill up all the holes
In my heart with what's true.
Then I can see clearly
What's old and not new.

From switching of lanes
To narrow the way,
To see the true cause
For this long delay.

When detours abound
On roads I don't know,
Then I must follow
The One who will show.

A season of change
Will soon come to be.
When all is finished
Then I can roam free.

The old is made new
On roads that go through.
To where I am going —
A beautiful view!

Resistance

Why is it so hard to enter this place?
A place so sweet — His welcome embrace.

The enemy comes to steal and destroy,
To take from this time what could be such joy.

Sometimes, I'm scared, but why all this fear
To meet with this One — treasured most dear?

Sometimes, it's life that pulls me to sway;
Things that must happen, I then go their way.

Sometimes, the world with all its display,
Draws me to follow, leads me away.

Sometimes, my past creeps into this place
Before I notice the lies to replace.

Sometimes, I'm buried in busyness things;
How they creep in with effortless wings.

All this aside, today I will choose:
To enter, draw near. Resistance — you lose.

Now in this place, I quiet my heart
To clear out the way, to make a new start.

Resistance is fading, falling away;
Sharpen my focus, I must not delay.
Let me remember — today's a new day.

Pointed Pencils

Nothing so pointless
As pencils gone dull.
Leaving them hidden
Their purpose is null.

Life can be like this
When hidden away.
Pointless to follow,
Again a delay.

A sharpener's needed
So it can write —
Exposing the hidden,
Revealing graphite.

So is my life when
The sharpening comes;
The Word of God pierces
Removing the stub.

Sharpen the pencil;
Push all the way in;
Leave nothing behind.
It's where you begin.

Surrender to God
In daily prayer
Keeps me much sharper;
The point is prepared.

Daily the pencil
Comes into this place
Where it is needed —
Sharpening's embrace.

So here I am
Once again today;
Deep in Your Word —
Let it sharpen the way.

My point is ready —
To write God's display
For all to see clearly
His life — and obey.

Unoffendable

The words that you speak,
I hear them today.
What do you mean
By all that you say?

Here's what I hear,
Sounds like this to me:
Something is stirring,
And I disagree.

Choosing this way,
To let go and forgive,
Is always for better —
The way I must live.

Then, there are also
These things that you do —
That stir up my anger,
And trouble me, too.

Again, I must learn
To let these things go.
For holding them tight
Will not help me I know.

So here, once again,
I choose to forgive;
I know it is always
The way I must live.

Offense is so easy;
It comes in so quick.
Surrounding me here,
It just wants to stick.

Reframe my anger,
In God's great design —
Let me be humble;
To Your plan, I resign.

Now I am choosing
To let all things go,
To not let my anger
Continue to grow,
For Your way is better —
I know that I know!

Fully Alive

Feet fitted for the gospel of peace,
Bandaged and broken — what brings a release?

Walking the journey to wholeness and love,
Steps now are taken — sent from above.

Waters of healing, remove all the stain,
Bandages covering what has been pain.

Leaving the past and all that's behind.
What is the future You have in mind?

When all is removed and I come to arrive,
This journey will end when I'm fully alive!

The Word

The Word made flesh, dwelling within,
The Word He speaks; it's where I begin.
Near is the Word; I see it for me.
He draws it out so others can see.

The Word calls me out, *Come to the light*,
Shines in my heart, exposes the night.
Calls me to walk in Christ alone,
Shining the light — His glory is shown.

The Word is a treasure hidden within,
Grounded in truth; it brings me the win.
Deep in the Word, it's where I can find —
His *rhema* Word; it's how I'm defined.

The Word has power; it strengthens my heart,
Dividing my soul and spirit apart.
Piercing to know my thoughts within,
Calls me to walk where I've never been.

The Word is life, eternally known.
Where do I go but to Christ alone?
The Word's where I live on rock solid ground;
A firm place to stand and where I am found.

The Word gives me strength from deep within
Even when battles tempt me to sin.
Declaring His word aligns me again;
Praise and thanksgiving — repeat the Amen!

Lectio Divina

Divine reading speaks;
It brings to the light.
Words on the pages
God brings into sight.

Words for this day
That shimmer and glow.
What I must ponder
That help me to grow.

These words are the tools,
He brings to the light.
For me to now see
In places of night.

To go from this place
Of darkness to light,
Connected to Him
Where I am made right.

Each day I must ponder
His Word just for me.
The clear Word He speaks
So I can live free.

His still small voice calls;
It beckons to me —
Come here to listen.
Divine words I now see.

Reach Out and Touch Him

Reach out and touch Him with all of your might.
Run quickly to Him; He's not out of sight.
Press into Jesus; His presence is here.
Only His garment is needed to share.

How daring are you? Where's your faith within?
To reach out and touch the One who can win.
If only I touch, I know I will be
Forever without this sickness in me.

What is now standing in way of my gain?
What will bring victory and keep me from pain?
For now is the time I speak out what's true —
Jesus has power for this, I conclude!

Praise to the One who is living in me!
His nearness is here; He's all that I need.
In Him, I now know, it's what I believe;
His goodness and power, I now receive.

Reach out and touch Him; He's here by your side,
Stretch out your hand; you won't be denied.
Jesus is here, and His power is great.
Touched by His love, you'll forever be changed.

Vision of Victory

A great cloud of witnesses cheers you now on,
Surrounding you always, *Rise up and be strong*.
Each one has words to speak to your heart;
Open up wide for God's Word to impart.

Every promise He's given is yours to receive.
Here at the table — abundance, believe.
More than you ask or imagine to be,
Is yours for this time — just open and see.

Deep in your spirit, His fullness is there,
Even when you are not yet aware.
This is the treasure deep in your heart;
You have within you enough to start.

So now go forth; be blessed in your day.
Let Jesus lead you all of the way.
Hang onto every promise He's given;
Know in your heart that you are forgiven;
Walk now in victory — *this is your vision*.

www.ingramcontent.com/pod-product-compliance
Lightning Source LLC
Chambersburg PA
CBHW040152110726
48005CB00018B/2737